Simple
African &
Middle Eastern Cuisine

- A De Sales Book -

Simple African & Middle Eastern Cuisine

First published in Great Britain
in 2016 by Arima Publishing

www.arimapublishing.com

ISBN 978 1 84549 689 0

A catalogue record of this book is available from the British Library

While every effort has been made to ensure the accuracy of the information
contained in this book, in no circumstances can the publisher or the author
accept any legal responsibility or liability for any loss or damage arising
from any error in or omission from the information contained in this book,
or from the failure of the reader to properly and accurately follow any
instructions contained in the book.

arima publishing
ASK House, Northgate Avenue
Bury St Edmunds, Suffolk IP32 6BB
t: (+44) 01284 700321

www.arimapublishing.com

Contents

Starters

Main Courses

Desserts

Introduction

As the cradles of human evolution and civilisation, Africa and the Middle East have a vibrant, ancient culture that is too often ignored by the rest of the world. To better understand the 60 plus countries that make up this region you need to look beyond media headlines towards the daily lives of everyday people. And nowhere is this better expressed than in their rich, and complex cookery.

Through its international network of writers, First De Sales has delved deep into the interior of Africa and the Middle East to experience a cuisine that is poorly documented in comparison to other parts of the globe. Presented here are recipes from each and every part of this enormous area. Some of these will be familiar, while others are appearing in print for the first time but, as with other De Sales cookery guides, all the recipes are straightforward, easy to follow and use ingredients that will be locally available.

Many readers will already be familiar with some of the fragrant and spicy food that comes from North Africa and the eastern Mediterranean, not least because it has had a historical influence on European cookery. *Simple African and Middle Eastern Cuisine* includes dishes from these areas but also looks beyond the obvious to find recipes that have escaped the attention of the wider world.

So why not use your own kitchen to take a culinary tour across a part of the globe whose cookery is all too often overlooked? From the exotic, such as Head and Leg Soup and Bobotie, to the more familiar kebabs and tagines, in here is everything you need to experience the rich flavours of Africa and the Middle East in the comfort of your own home.

Bon Appétit!

Starters

Tripoli Lamb Soup
Libya

I worked in Libya after the start of the revolution, arriving in summer 2012 and departing in November 2014. I would love to go back but, sadly, this doesn't look likely. Libyan soup is very unusual and it has a taste like no other. Most local restaurants give you this soup whether you ask for it or not, and customers come to expect it everywhere. Lots of Mediterranean food is ubiquitous (lamb kebabs, humus, pitta bread) but you can only get Libyan soup in Libya.

Serves 6

2 tablespoons extra virgin olive oil • 300g of chopped onion • 230g boneless lamb shoulder or dark chicken meat, finely chopped • 4 medium-size ripe tomatoes, diced • 100g of tomato paste • 2 teaspoons sweet paprika • ½ teaspoon cayenne pepper or harissa, or to taste • ½ teaspoon saffron threads • Salt and freshly ground black pepper to taste • 100g of fine pearl barley or couscous (barley is best) • 100g of cooked chickpeas, drained (canned are fine) • 1 tablespoon finely chopped cilantro leaves (lime leaves can be used) • 1 tablespoon finely chopped flat-leaf parsley leaves • ½ tablespoon dried mint • 1.8 litres water

Heat the oil in a large casserole or saucepan. Add the onion and lamb (or chicken) and cook for about five minutes, stirring frequently, until just beginning to brown.

Add the tomatoes, tomato paste, paprika, cayenne (or harissa), saffron, salt and pepper. Stir, then add 1.8 litres of water. Bring to a simmer and cook for 45 minutes.

Add the barley (or couscous) and chickpeas and cook for a further 15 minutes, until the barley is tender. Add the cilantro (or lime leaves) and parsley. Taste and adjust salt and cayenne. Add dried mint. Cook for five minutes, then serve.

Chef's Tip
This soup make's and ideal lunch or it can be served as a starter. I recommend serving it with butter and fresh bread.

Desert Salad
Egypt

This healthy option is perfect to share as a side plate, starter or light lunch. I was introduced to this dish by Sheriti, a wonderful Egyptian girl whom I used to know. I never really saw the appeal of meat and fish free dishes, but her energy and zest for life was convincing enough for me to give this a try, and it didn't take long for this to become a regular fixture in my day-to-day diet.

Serves 2
1 small red onion • 300g baby plum tomatoes • 125g fat mozzarella • 1 ripe avocado • 1 tablespoon olive oil • ½ tablespoon balsamic vinegar • Splash of lemon juice

Finely chop the red onion and half the baby tomatoes. Place them in a salad bowl.

Take the mozzarella and tear it into bite-sized pieces. Add it to the bowl.

Slice the avocado but not too finely. It should have a chunky appearance. Add this to the bowl.

In an old jam jar or other suitable container, add the olive oil, vinegar and lemon juice. Shake or stir vigorously until the ingredients are mixed. Pour over the salad and gently toss. The salad is ready to serve.

Chef's Tip
For a bit more of a kick, add a half teaspoon of English or French mustard to the dressing and then shake well. Reduced fat mozzarella can be used by those who are calorie conscious.

Kirmizi Mercimek Corbasi: Red Lentil Soup
Turkey

I think that lentils are an under appreciated food in much of Europe, perhaps because they are associated with vegetarian and vegan food. Across the Middle East lentils are a staple part of the diet and are used in a variety of dishes to add protein, taste and texture. This creamy soup is popular in Turkey and is colourful, tasty and simple to make. To those who have yet to learn to love the lentil, this will be a perfect introduction.

Serves 2
**125g red lentils, cleaned and washed • 1 litre beef stock •
2 tablespoons butter or margarine • 2 tablespoons wheat
flour • 1 onion • Pinch of salt**

Cut the onion into small slices and put them into a saucepan with a tablespoon of butter. Place over a medium heat and cook for ten minutes or until the onion is glazed. Be careful not to let it burn.

Add the beef stock, lentils and salt. Bring the mixture to boil for a short period and turn down so that it simmers for around 30 to 40 minutes.

Let the mixture cool for ten minutes then either roughly blend the mixture (a hand blender is good for this) or (for a more traditional texture) press the lentils through a coarse sieve.

In another small saucepan, heat up a tablespoon of butter. When melted add the flour and stir it in. Keep stirring until it starts to turn golden brown.

Immediately add the blended lentils and increase the heat until it boils. Stir regularly to prevent burning. Once boiling, the mixture is ready to serve in bowls.

Serve the soup with gratin bread (roasted cubic bread) and with a garnish of coriander leaves.

Chef's Tip
This soup is usually served before a meal with a dollop of yogurt or tzatiki sauce swirled in.

Tarhana Corbasi: Tarhana Soup
Turkey

This recipes was given to me by a family friend. His parents were originally from the Middle East and over the years he and his wife have served some of the dishes as part of their informal family occasions. My wife requested the recipe and it has become part of our family occasions too – our children are all grown now but these simple dishes evoke many happy memories.

Serves 4
500g <u>each</u> of red and green peppers, onions and tomatoes • 500g yoghurt • Plain flour • 1 litre beef stock • 100g minced beef or lamb • 80g tarhana mass (see below) • 1 tablespoon butter/margarine • 2 tomatoes, skinned and cut in cubes • 1 teaspoon tomato purée and some salt

You can buy tarhana mass in Turkish supermarkets but it is better to make it yourself, as follows.

Take the red and green pepper, onions and tomatoes and boil them in water until soft. Take the vegetables from the heat, sieve and blend to a paste. When it has cooled down a little bit, add the yoghurt and stir.

Add small amounts of plain flour and stir into the mixture until a thickened mass is formed. Then add some salt to taste as desired. Spread the mixture on a flat tray in a 2 cm thick layer. Cover and leave for one to two days.

Once set, break the tarhana into small pieces and leave it to air-dry on some clean tea towels. When dry, hand-rub these into small pieces and store in small containers to be used when needed.

For the soup. Heat the butter in a saucepan and add the minced meat. Fry for ten minutes.

Add the tomato purée, beef stock and the tomato cubes. Boil it all together and then mix in the tarhana mass. Bring it to the boil again, stirring continuously. Serve it hot with croutons, if desired.

Chef's Tip
To enhance the flavour try adding two or three small pieces of Garlic to the soup.

Paca Corbasi: Head and Leg Soup
Turkey

Don't let the name of this delicious soup put you off. Yes, you can cook it using a whole head but this is admittedly not everyone's cup of tea so luckily it is equally as delicious using more conventional meat products. Hot and savoury, this is an easy dish to cook and a great talking piece at any dinner party.

Serves 4
6 lamb or calf legs or a head • 1.5 litres water • 100g butter • 2 tablespoons plain flour • Pinch of Salt • Pinch of hot chilli pepper • 100ml vinegar • 4 pieces garlic

Boil the Legs and head in 1.5 litres of water for two hours. Strain, retaining the water as the base of the soup. Separate the meat from the bone, cutting it into small cubes. Discard the bones.

Put the meat back into the saucepan. The garlic pieces need to be crushed, mixed with the vinegar, and put into the soup base.

In another small saucepan, heat up 50 grams of butter, add the flour and cook until gold brown. Then mix in a few tablespoons of the soup base.

Melt the rest of the butter, mix with the chilli pepper and then add it to the soup base. Heat thoroughly and add salt and pepper according to taste. Serve immediately.

Chef's Tip
This is best served with Turkish ramazan bread but if this is not available then a plain Indian naan bread makes a good substitute.

Pharaoh's Feast: Egyptian Omelette
Egypt

Tasty and filling, this recipe can be adapted to cater for different tastes and preferences by adding or subtracting meat, vegetables and various cheeses. This recipe was the original one given to me but I have made many adaptations from it – all of them successfully!

Serves 4
8 free range eggs, lightly beaten • 1 large onion, sliced • 1 large garlic clove, crushed • 1 tablespoon butter • ½ teaspoon dried mixed herbs • 250g cooked chicken • 1 medium-sized aubergine or tomatoes • 1 tablespoon olive oil • 155g cooked pasta • Pinch of black ground pepper

Firstly thinly slice the aubergine and place in strainer. It is not necessary to peel the aubergine but this can be done if preferred. Lightly sprinkle the aubergine with salt and put to one side for approximately 30 minutes. When the time is up, shake off any excess moisture and pat dry with some kitchen roll.

If possible use an omelette pan but any good quality heavy bottom frying pan works equally well.

On a low heat melt the butter and oil and gently sauté the onion and garlic for approximately 2 minutes.

Keeping heat low add the aubergine and cook slowly until softened (or add tomatoes).

Add the cooked meat and pasta and sprinkle in the dried herbs.

Pour the egg mixture into a frying pan and add ground pepper to taste. Stir mixture all together and leave to cook through.

When almost set place under hot grill to finish cooking the top of omelette and to brown it slightly.

Can be served immediately as hot dish or left to cool and cut into wedges.

Chef's Tip
Serve with fresh salad and crusty bread – also ideal for picnics and lunch boxes.

Quick and Easy Hummus
Algeria

This recipe has been adapted to make it quicker and easier than some of the more traditional ways of create hummus but it is delicious all the same. I have found that hummus is especially popular at children's birthday parties where it can be enjoyed by both adults and children alike. It also makes a great starter, snack or side dish.

Serves 4
1 can chickpeas, drained and rinsed • 5 tablespoons olive oil • 2 tablespoons fresh lemon juice • 1 tablespoon crushed garlic • 1 teaspoon ground cumin • ½ teaspoon paprika • 2 tablespoons of tahini, optional • Pinch of sea salt

Place all ingredients except the paprika in a food processor until smooth and creamy. Water can be added until correct consistency reached.

To look authentic place hummus into decorative brightly coloured bowl and drizzle extra olive oil on top and sprinkle with paprika.

This delicious and nutritious dip can be served with vegetable crudités and lightly toasted pitta bread.

Chef's Tip
Tahini is a sesame seed paste which is not essential to the recipe but it does add to the authenticity of this dish.

Afelia: Pork Belly Stew
Lebanon

Afelia is normally cooked in a 'tava' (earthenware dish) placed inside a traditional clay oven. It is commonly eaten in many parts of the Middle East and is also found in Greece and Cyprus. If possible use a wine from the region rather than the cheapest supermarket brand.

Serves 4

1kg pork belly, cubed (fillet can be used for a leaner finish) • 6 teaspoons coriander seeds • 4 tablespoons olive oil • 2 large onions, sliced • 300ml red wine • salt and pepper • ½ teaspoon cinnamon

Crush the coriander seeds as finely as possible in a pestle and mortar. In a large pot add these to the pork together with the wine. Season with salt and pepper, cover and marinate for at least four hours, or overnight in the fridge.

Preheat the oven to 160°C. Drain the meat but save the marinade.

Heat half the oil and fry the meat in small batches to brown then transfer to a casserole dish.

In the same pan as you fried the meat, heat the remaining oil and fry the onions and cinnamon over a medium heat until soft and translucent. Add the wine marinade an bring to a simmer.

Pour this mixture over the meat and cover. Cook in the oven for up to 3 hours (fillet will take less). Serve with a green salad and rice.

Chef's Tip
This stew also goes well with boiled vegetables such as potatoes and carrots. It is a good alternative to a Sunday roast on a cold winter's day.

Falafel: Chickpea Fritters
Arabia - traditional

The falafel is a common sight in takeaways and supermarkets, and is popular as a vegetarian alternative on restaurant menus. This dish was introduced into Europe from the Middle East in the 1970s and has become widespread. Manufactured falafels have a certain charm but cannot beat the taste and texture of the real thing. Try the recipe below and I am sure you will agree with me.

For 8-10 Falafels
400g tin of chickpeas, drained • 1 small red onion, roughly chopped • 2 or 3 cloves of garlic • 1½ tablespoons plain flour • ¼ teaspoon salt • 1 teaspoon ground cumin • 1 teaspoon ground coriander • 1 tsp chilli powder • ¼ teaspoon ground black pepper • Fresh parsley and mint, to taste • Vegetable oil

Pulse the garlic and onion in a food processor and blend until finely chopped.

Add all the other ingredients (except the oil) and blend until they are all thoroughly combined. You will need to scrape the sides of the processor to make sure any lumps get brought into the mix. You want the mix fairly fine but a few small lumps of chickpeas are nice for texture.

Shape the mixture into 8 to 10 evenly-sized balls. Gently flatten these into patties then refrigerate for around an hour to firm up.

Heat a few tablespoons of vegetable oil in a frying pan and cook the balls on a medium heat for 2 to 3 minutes on each side, until crisp and browned. Remove with a slotted spoon and drain on kitchen paper.

Chef's Tip
Serve in either pitta or flat breads with salad, chilli sauce and yoghurt if desired. They may be eaten hot or cold.

Fasolada: Bean Soup
Cyprus/Lebanon

This is a family recipe. It is a wholesome starter, or can be used as a main meal in bigger portions and accompanied with bread or chicken, although serving with sardines or mackerel is best. This is sometimes referred to as being the national dish of Greece but it is also eaten in some of the Middle Eastern countries with a Mediterranean coastline. Despite its widespread popularity, this is a dish that is rarely seen in restaurants.

Serves 8

**½ kg dried cannelini beans • 120ml of sunflower oil •
60ml of olive oil • 1 large onion, finely chopped • 3 celery
sticks, chopped • 3 carrots, diced • 1 tin of finely chopped/
blended tomatoes • 2 teaspoons of fresh, chopped parsley
• Salt and pepper to taste**

Soak the beans in water overnight; this is very important. Change the water and boil the beans for approximately 30 minutes. Add chopped carrots and celery; bring back to the boil

Add in the onion and then the blended tomato. Add both the sunflower oil and olive oil. Bring back to the boil and add the celery and parsley plus the salt and pepper.

Leave everything to simmer for at least half an hour. Check it is ready by testing the beans - if they are soft, then serve.

Chef's Tip
Make as much as you like, as it keeps really well and is arguably even better the next day as the soup thickens over time.

Kachumbari: Spicy Salsa Salad
Tanzania

This simple, frugal and sometimes spicy salad or salsa is eaten all over East Africa but with regional variations. I acquired this version from my mother-in-law. It is a refreshing, tasty accompaniment to meaty dishes and can be prepared in next to no time. I often turn to this when we're short for time or when the fridge is on the empty side! Traditionally Tanzanians use pili pili kicha (literally 'crazy chilli') which are small, incredibly spicy, red chillies, but you could also substitute these for scotch bonnets or jalapeño.

Serves 4
500g large plum tomatoes • 1 or 2 small red onions •
Half a cucumber (optional) • 1 large carrot (optional) • 2
tablespoons of fresh, finely chopped coriander (optional)
• 1 or 2 small red chillies • Juice of 1 lemon • A pinch of
salt

Finely slice all the vegetables and place them in a bowl. Finely chop and then lightly pound the chillies with the salt with a pestle and mortar.

Mix the chilli and salt mixture with the lemon juice. Drizzle the lemon/chilli dressing over the chopped vegetables. Scatter over the coriander and serve. This salad is best eaten a few hours after preparation when the juices have mingled and the flavours have been drawn out.

Chef's Tip
If you find raw onions too strong, their pungency can be reduced by placing the sliced onions in a bowl, adding a pinch of salt and then boiling water to cover the onions.

Pili Pili: Chilli Dipping Sauce
Tanzania

Most Tanzanians can't do without this quick, easy and fresh dipping sauce. Usually eaten as an accompaniment to barbecued meat (especially goat and beef), plantains, chips, fish or chicken it could be used as a dipping sauce or condiment for practically anything. My wife often likes to slurp it straight off the spoon! It makes use of the pili pili 'crazy chillies' but scotch bonnets or jalapeños can work just as well. There are many variations of this dipping sauce, here is my favourite.

Serves 2
4 to 5 plum tomatoes • 1 or 2 small red chillies; scotch bonnet, jalapeño or pili pili kichaa • Juice of 1 lemon • 2 or 3 cloves of garlic (to taste) • A good handful of fresh coriander • A pinch of salt (or to taste)

Roughly chop the tomatoes and finely chop the garlic. Carefully chop the chillies into fine pieces; be careful not to get the chillies on your fingers or, if you do, scrub them afterwards and don't touch your eyes or lips.

Add everything to a food processor and blitz until liquid. The sauce should turn slightly pink and frothy. Taste and add more salt/lemon juice/chillies if required and blitz again. Serve as is or chilled.

For a smoother sauce try halving the tomatoes length wise and then grating the cut half against the large sized grater. Discard the skins before blitzing the grated tomato with the rest of the ingredients.

Chef's Tip
Try to use ripe, red tomatoes, preferably at room temperature. Only use fresh chillies and garlic.

Tabouleh: Bulgur Wheat Salad
Arabia

This vegetarian recipe is simple to prepare but filling to eat. The taste is sharp, fresh and aromatic and will leave your palate refreshed. The perfect summer treat.

Serves 4
**45g fine bulgur wheat • 1 large bunch flat leaf parsley,
chopped • 1 small bunch of mint leaves, chopped • 4 sweet
plum tomatoes, quartered • 1 small onion or 3 shallots,
cubed • 150g feta cheese, chopped • Juice from 1 lemon •
1 large tablespoon of virgin olive oil • 1 teaspoon of salt**

Place the bulgur wheat into a small bowl and cover with 50ml of boiling water. Stir and set aside for 20 minutes or until the Bulgur wheat has absorbed all of the water. Fluff it using a fork until the grains are separated.

In a big salad bowl put the bulgur wheat, tomatoes, onions, chopped parsley and mint. Gently mix together, being careful not to squash the tomatoes

Sprinkle on the feta cheese. Drizzle over the olive oil, lemon juice and salt. Mix well to coat all the ingredients. Serve on its own or with a grilled flat bread.

Chef's Tip
This dish can be prepared ahead of time and kept in the fridge. It is deal for lunches and picnics.

Main Courses

Guvec Kebabi: Lamb Casserole
Turkey

This traditional Turkish dish ideally requires an earthenware pot with a lid but if all else fails then a normal casserole dish will do (but don't soak it in water). This recipe is popular in Turkey and can be found in many restaurants there. I like it because it takes a short time to prepare and then can be left to cook while I get on with other things.

Serves 4
**1 kg lamb leg, cut into cubes • 250g onions, cut into cubes
• 2 tablespoons butter • 3 tomatoes • 150 g mixed peppers
• 6 to 8 small pieces garlic, crushed • 1 teaspoon thyme •
salt, black pepper, and chilli pepper, according to taste**

Preheat the oven to 175°C. Soak the clay pot (guvec) in water for 15 minutes. Rub the inside of the pot with a mix of salted garlic and butter.

Mix the meat with rest of the ingredients and place into the clay pot. Cover the pot and put it into the oven for 60 to 90 minutes. Remove from the oven and serve with rice and salad!

Chef's Tip
For those that are fans of slow cookers, this recipe is ideal. The lamb should emerge juicy and tender.

Sweet and Sour Fish
Persia

Most children are not keen on fish but do often have a sweet tooth. This dish uses fruit juices to add the sweetness which is healthy and tasty.

Serves 4

150g washed and chopped spring onions • 2 cloves garlic, peeled and crushed • 120ml oil • 240ml of pomegranate juice or 1 tablespoon pomegranate paste dissolved in 120ml water • 240ml orange juice • 120ml cup of lemon juice • 240ml tomato juice • 1 teaspoon salt • 1 tablespoon honey or sugar • 4 thick fish fillets, cod, trout or sea bass - washed and pat dried • 2 big tablespoons of flour

In a saucepan, heat the oil, fry the scallions and garlic. Add pomegranate, tomato, lemon and orange juice. Add half a teaspoon salt. Stir and bring to the boil, taste, add honey or sugar (if necessary).

Preheat the oven to 230°C. Mix half a teaspoon of salt and all the flour together in a bowl and sprinkle over both sides of the fish. In a frying pan, gently heat some oil and lightly fry the fish on both sides taking care not to burn.

Place the fried fish in an ovenproof dish. Pour the sauce over the fish, cover with foil, and bake for 5-10 minutes. Remove from the oven and serve immediately.

Chef's Tip
Garnish with a few pomegranate seeds and serve with steamed vegetables or rice.

Spicy Lamb Kebabs
Algeria

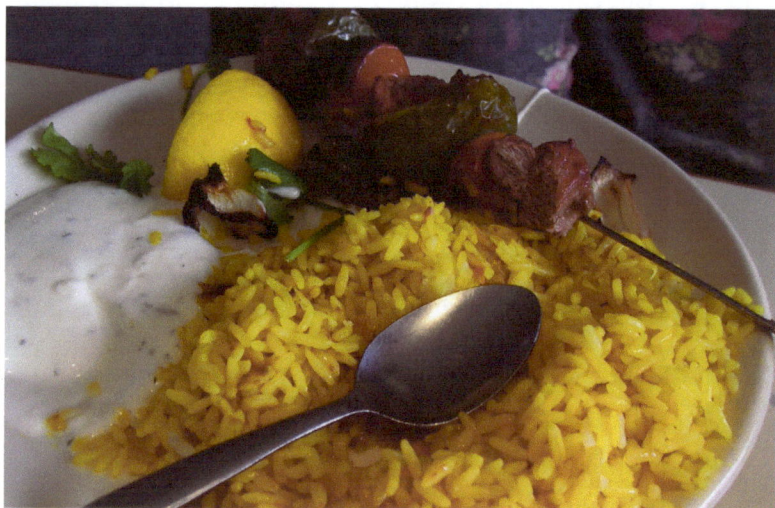

I first came across this recipe travelling in Algeria in the early 1970s. You could buy the kebabs from street sellers who would ease the meat into warm bread for eating immediately. Kebabs are ideal for a barbecue, but are equally delicious under the grill. If you are missing one or two of the spices, don't worry too much as the meat will still be tasty. The bitterness of the limes is a good contrast with the sweetness of the meat, but if you prefer, put pieces of red, green or yellow peppers between the lamb chunks for colour.

Serves 4

750g lamb • 1 lemon • 150ml olive oil • ½ tablespoon of coriander • 2 cloves of garlic, crushed • ½ tablespoon of turmeric • 1 teaspoon of ground ginger • ½ tablespoon of cumin • 2 bay leaves, crushed • one glass of red wine • salt and freshly ground black pepper added to taste • 2 limes cut into segments rather than slices or if you prefer sections of red, green, yellow pepper

The kebabs are best prepared 8-12 hours in advance to allow the marinade to work its way into the meat, bur shorter marinating time will still give you a good result. Preparing the marinade should take no more than about twenty minutes with another ten for cutting the meat into cubes. Once the kebabs are on the barbecue or under the grill, they will take about 8 minutes to cook.

Trim off any fat from the lamb and cut it into regular-sized cubes of about 3-5cm. Mix the marinade of lemon juice, olive oil, wine, coriander, garlic, turmeric, ginger, cumin, bay leaves, salt and pepper in a bowl.

Put the meat into the bowl and stir so that the marinade coats all of the meat. Cover the bowl and keep in the refrigerator until ready for cooking.

Drain the marinade and keep to one side. Make sure that your hands are clean and then thread the meat onto skewers using the wedges of lime or pepper between the chunks of lamb. This can be a messy business so make sure that your clothes are protected.

Put the skewers onto a preheated barbecue using the marinade as a barbecue sauce, brushing the meat frequently. Turn the meat to ensure that it is cooked on all sides. Cooking the meat will take about 8 minutes, but make sure that the pieces at the end of the skewer are heated all the way through. Some people prefer the meat slightly red in the middle, this is a matter of taste, but whatever your preference, this dish is best not overcooked.

Chef's Tip
Serve with hot pitta bread (it can be heated on the barbecue at the same time as the meat) or boiled rice.

Bobotie: African Curry
South Africa

A hot warming main course which fills the kitchen with a wonderful aroma. I was introduced to this dish whilst I was a medical student working in a mission hospital in rural Transvaal. One of the doctors there working on National Service used his mother's recipe for what is a traditional South African dish. I've since discovered that it probably arrived there with Malaysian immigrants during the 17th century. It consists of a complex mix of flavours, textures and styles. The heat, tartness and sweet flavours combine to seduce everyone who tastes it.

Serves 4
2 tablespoons vegetable oil • 2 medium onions, chopped • 2 slices white bread soaked in milk, squeezed dry and crumbled • 750g finely minced lamb (or beef) • 1 tablespoon ground ginger • 1 tablespoon brown sugar • 4 teaspoons curry powder • 1 tablespoon turmeric •

salt and freshly ground pepper • 2 tablespoons mango chutney • 50g raisins • 100g blanched almonds • 60g chopped granny smith or other tart apple • juice of 1 lemon • 1 tablespoon apricot jam • 2 tablespoons tomato paste • 1 egg

Topping
300ml milk • 2 eggs • pinch of salt • 1 teaspoon grated lemon rind

Preheat oven to 120ºC. Heat oil in a sauté pan over medium heat. Add onions and sauté until softened (about 3 minutes). Add curry powder, ginger and turmeric and cook until fragrant (about 1 minute). Add ground beef and sauté for 2 minutes or until it starts to lose its pinkness.

Combine the meat mixture in a large, flameproof casserole with the bread, brown sugar, lemon juice, chutney, half of the chopped almonds, raisins, apple, 1 egg , apricot jam and tomato paste and season with salt and pepper. Mix well, over a medium heat. Bake uncovered in the oven for 30 minutes. Press down the mixture.

Mix together the 2 remaining eggs, the reserved milk and the lemon rind and pour over the meat mixture. Decorate with onion rings and extra almonds.

Raise the oven temperature to 180ºC and bake for an additional 45 minutes. Serve with long grain rice flavoured with turmeric and cinnamon.

Chef's Tip
Many variations of ingredients are possible for this eclectic dish. Try apricots instead of raisins, or individual spices instead of curry powder.

Lemon Chicken Tagine
Morocco

I am an extremely well-travelled gourmet but until recently had not experienced Moroccan food. On holiday in the village of Moraira on the Spanish Costa Blanca I tried a small restaurant specialising in Moroccan dishes. It turned out the restaurant is run by a Moroccan husband and wife team and thus truly authentic dishes are on offer. The Moroccan lamb tagine and lemon chicken are delicious and after a couple of visits to the restaurant I managed to persuade the owner to part with the two recipe set out below.

Serves 4

1.5kg whole chicken • 50g chicken livers chopped • 100g butter • confit of 1 lemon • 2 onions finely chopped • 4 cloves of garlic crushed • ¾ teaspoon turmeric • ¾ teaspoon saffron strands • 1 tablespoon ground ginger • 100g Kalamata olives • 2 tablespoons fresh chopped coriander • 2 tablespoons fresh chopped parsley • salt and pepper

Put the chicken into a flameproof casserole, tagine or saucepan in which it fits tightly. Add the onion, garlic, butter, ginger, turmeric and saffron; season. Pour in 700ml water, cover and bring to the boil over a medium to high heat. Reduce the heat and leave to simmer, spooning the sauce over the chicken and turning it over now and then until it is just cooked through – about 40 minutes. Lift the chicken onto a plate and cover with foil.

Add the lemon juice to the casserole, increase the heat once more and simmer the sauce rapidly until reduced by about two-thirds. Return the chicken to the casserole with the olives and pieces of preserved lemon, cover with a well-fitting lid and simmer for a further 20–25 minutes until the chicken is tender. Lift the chicken onto a large, warmed platter.

Add the chicken liver to the sauce and simmer for 5 minutes. Add the herbs and adjust the seasoning if necessary. Spoon the sauce over the chicken and serve.

Chef's Tip
Traditionally this would be served with bread alone but it would also be good served with couscous.

Spicy Tamarind Trout
Persia

I love fish and hot food but was never very keen on fish curry so my wife came up with this dish which I love.

Serves 4
4 trout medium-sized (gutted) • 1 clove garlic • 1
teaspoon tamarind paste • 250g coriander • 250g parsley
• 2 hot chillies • ¼ teaspoon salt • Cajun seasoning
(optional)

Wash the fish and leave so the excess water can drain. Peel and crush the garlic. Wash and chop the coriander and parsley. Wash and chop chillies. Mix the chopped coriander, parsley, chilli, crushed garlic, salt and tamarind paste in a bowl. Stuff the fish with the mixture.

Heat the oven to 230°C. Place a large piece of foil on a baking tray, enough to cover the fish when folded over. Oil the foil (to avoid sticking).

Place the fish in the tray and cover with aluminium foil. Cook for 15-20 minutes at 230°C. Serve the fish whole on a serving dish and garnish with some parsley.

Chef's Tip
Steamed rice or boiled potatoes would be a good accompaniment.

Chicken Tagine
Tunisia

This recipe will be familiar to anyone who has holidayed in Tunisia. It is a classic dish that will evoke visions of deserts, palm trees and cities with minarets. More importantly, it is relatively healthy and filling and tastes great.

Serves 4
**4 chicken thighs • 10g butter or olive oil • 1 teaspoon
ground ginger • 1 teaspoon cinnamon • 1 teaspoon
saffron • ½ teaspoon cayenne pepper • 1 teaspoon
turmeric • 1 large onion, grated • 550ml chicken stock •
100g large olives • 1 lemon, sliced.**

Place the chicken thighs in a heavy saucepan or casserole dish with a lid. Add some oil and then fry until the chicken is cooked and brown. Remove the chicken and set aside.

Add the onion and spices to the pan and fry until the onion is soft. Put the chicken back in with the stock and bring to the boil. Reduce the heat and simmer for around 30 minutes.

Remove the chicken and boil the stock to reduce it. When sufficiently thickened, return the chicken to the pan together with the olives and lemon. Heat thoroughly and then serve with couscous or rice.

Chef's Tip
It is worth spending a bit more to get free range or, better still, organic chicken pieces. You will notice the difference in taste and so will your family and dinner guests.

Ruz Kabsa: Savoury Chicken and Rice
Saudi Arabia

I discovered this simple dish at a local restaurant while in the Middle East on business and this is my attempt at reproducing it. I have always enjoyed discovering different foods when abroad and always remember the old Middle eastern saying that 'our health is our wealth'.

Serves 4

½ teaspoon saffron • ¼ teaspoon ground cardamom • ½ teaspoon cinnamon • ½ teaspoon all spice • ½ teaspoon white pepper • ½ teaspoon lime powder • 60g butter • 1 small onion, finely chopped • 6 cloves garlic, crushed • 1.4kgs chicken, cut into 8 pieces • 4 tablespoons tomato puree • 400g chopped tomatoes • 3 carrots peeled and grated • 2 whole cloves • 1 pinch ground nutmeg • 1 pinch ground cumin • 1 pinch ground coriander • Salt and black pepper to taste • 700ml hot water • 1 chicken stock cube • 500g basmati rice • 115g raisins • 115g slivered almonds, toasted

In a small bowl mix together the saffron, cardamom, cinnamon, allspice, white pepper and lime powder. This is the kabsa spice mix. Set aside.

Melt the butter in a large casserole pot over a medium heat. Stir in the garlic and onion. Fry and stir for five minutes until the onion has softened and turned translucent. Add the chicken pieces and brown them over medium high heat. This will take about 10 minutes. Mix in the tomato puree.

Stir in the canned tomatoes, grated carrots, whole cloves, nutmeg, cumin, coriander, salt, black pepper and the kabsa spice mix. Cook for about three minutes, pour in the water and add the chicken bouillon cube.

Bring the sauce to a boil, then reduce the heat to simmer and cover the Pot. Simmer until the chicken is no longer pink and the juices run clear. This will take about 30 minutes.

Gently stir in the rice. Cover the pot and then simmer for about 25 minutes until the rice is tender and almost dry. Add the raisins and a little more hot water, if necessary. Cover and cook for an additional five to ten minutes or until the rice grains have separated.

Transfer the rice to a large platter and arrange the chicken pieces on top. Sprinkle the toasted almonds over the dish and serve at once.

Chef's Tip
Serve with a fresh salad, little lime vinaigrette and some fresh pita breads. Saudi people like their kasba with a hot sauce called shattah.

Kuku Paka: Hot Chicken Stew
Tanzania

By far and away one of my favourite East African dishes – preferably eaten round a camp fire with an ice cold beer after a day's safari. Simple, tasty and a little bit fiery, if you like it like that.

Serves 4
4 large chicken breasts halved and then cut into strips •
170g cream of coconut in a coffee mug of warm water •
1 teaspoon salt • 1 teaspoon ground ginger • 1 teaspoon
garlic • 60g grated tomato • ½ teaspoons turmeric
powder • ½ teaspoon ground black pepper • 1 tablespoon
squeezed lemon juice • 2 tablespoons freshly chopped
coriander • 1 or 2 finely chopped chillies

Take a non-stick pan or wok and add the chicken strips, half the salt, chillies and tomatoes. Stir and then add all the garlic, turmeric and ground pepper plus a small amount of water to moisten. Then slow cook on low heat with the pan covered. If needed, add more water.

Into a separate, smaller non-stick pan, add coconut milk, the rest of the chillies, tomato and salt. Bring to the boil and simmer for six or seven minutes or until the mixture thickens. Once at desired texture remove from the heat.

Pour the coconut mixture over the cooked chicken, mix well and then bring to the boil. Simmer on low heat for a further three or four minutes. Add the lemon juice.

Serve with rice – simple boiled rice is my favourite but anything goes.

Chef's Tip
Another favourite for me is to eat it using poppadums rather than a fork.

Boerewars: South African Sausages
South Africa

If there's one country that's protein hungry and meat crazy it has to be South Africa. A trip over there could have you eating all sorts of different meats from ostrich to crocodile, impala to kudu or just a humble beef steak. When I travelled out there it was BBQs every night with rack upon rack of cooked tender meat... and the odd lettuce leaf for show! Boerewars are a South African favourite and recipes are normally handed down through the generations – this one came from a family I stayed with in Johannesburg.

You will need a mincer to have a go at making these and don't get too stressed about the result as by the time you get it on the BBQ you will probably have had a couple of beers anyway.

Serves 4
**2kg matured and tenderised beef • 1kg belly pork • 90g
thick sausage casing soaked in water to soften • 35ml
coriander seeds • 10 cloves whole • 30ml salt • 15ml
ground black pepper • 2ml nutmeg grated • 10ml allspice
ground • 10ml brown sugar • 125ml dry red wine • Splash
of dark vinegar**

Cut the white stringy bits off the beef. Cut the beef and pork into strips and mince through the mincer. In a small frying pan roast the coriander and cloves until brown.

Grind the roasted spices with a pestle and mortar before mixing with the salt, pepper, nutmeg and allspice. Add the sugar. Once all the spices are mixed thoroughly add them to the mince. Then add the red wine and a splash of vinegar.

Place the sausage funnel over the end of the mincer. Take the sausage casing out of the water and place one end over the funnel. Then push all of the casing on, to leave about five or eight centimetres dangling down. Tie this off.

Feed the mixture through the grinder and into the casing, a little at a time, moulding the growing sausage with your hands. Once all the mixture has been used, remove the casing from the mincer funnel and knot the end. Cook on a BBQ.

Chef's Tip
Filling the sausage cases is a job that is best done with two people.

Za'atar Chicken
Lebanon

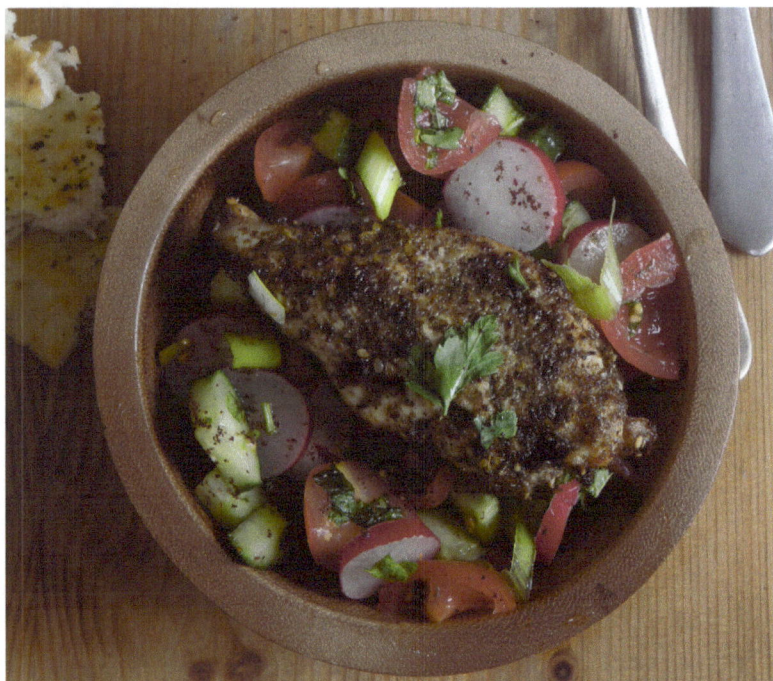

This is a Middle Eastern dish that is packed with flavour but has something of a fresh kick from the use of lemon and lime. Simple but tasty - you can't go wrong!

Serves 4
4 large chicken breasts • 3 large onions, peeled and sliced • 1 red pepper, sliced into strips • 1 green pepper, sliced into strips • 2 tablespoons of olive oil mixed with 1 tablespoon of za'atar mixture (see below).

For the marinade
Juice 1 lemon (plus wedges to decorate) • Juice 1 lime (plus wedges to decorate) • Fresh black pepper and salt to taste • 4 teaspoons of garlic

For the Za'atar
**4 teaspoons dried marjoram • 4 teaspoons sesame seeds •
4 teaspoons dried thyme • 4 teaspoons ground cumin • 4
teaspoons ground sumac • 4 tablespoons fresh oregano •
1 teaspoon sea salt**

To make the za'atar. Gently toast the sesame seeds on a low heat in a dry pan and then add these to the other ingredients. Place everything in blender until finely mixed. This can be stored in an airtight container in the fridge for up to a week.

Place the chicken pieces in a roasting tin. Mix the marinade ingredients of lemon/lime juice, garlic and salt together and pour over the chicken. Cover with clingfilm and leave in fridge for approximately 2 hours.

Preheat the oven to 200°C. When the time is up remove the chicken from the roasting dish and spread the sliced onion and peppers over the base. Sprinkle the za'atar mixture over the onions and peppers and place the chicken pieces back on top of them. Glaze the chicken portions with the olive oil mixture and place in the oven.

Roast for approximately 45 minutes or until chicken is thoroughly cooked. Serve with seasonal side vegetables and fragrant rice and decorate with lemon and lime wedges which have been lightly grilled for colour.

Chef's Tip
Za'atar can be bought from many Middle Eastern shops and can be sprinkled over flat breads or potato wedges for a tasty side dish.

Mandi Chicken
Yemen

This is a simplified version of a traditional Yemeni dish but without the burning coal stage. It is delicious all the same.

Serves 4
4 chicken halves • 150-200g basmati rice • 1 large de-seeded chopped tomato • 1 tablespoon butter • 1 large onion • 1 teaspoon garlic purée • 4 whole cardamom pods • 6 whole cloves • 6 black peppercorns • 1 tablespoon of coriander powder (optional) • 550ml chicken stock • 1 teaspoon sea salt • 1 teaspoon olive oil • Sliced almonds, for decoration)

For the spiced mix you will need
4 bay leaves • 2 teaspoons black ground pepper • 2
teaspoons turmeric • 1 teaspoon ground nutmeg • 2
tablespoons cloves • 2 tablespoons cardamom pods • 1
tablespoon ground ginger

Place all spiced mix ingredients into blender until finely crushed. Rub the spice mix all over the chicken pieces and leave to marinade (in fridge) for at least 2 hours.

Place oil in frying pan and cook chicken (uncovered) on low heat for about 30 to 40 minutes until tender and brown. Then set aside but keep warm.

Add butter to pan and gently sauté onions and garlic until golden. Add rice and other remaining ingredients and also stock and bring to boil. Reduce heat and add chopped tomato. Cover with lid and simmer for about 20 to 30 minutes until rice cooked and liquid reduced.

Fluff rice (add knob of butter if required) and place chicken pieces on top. Sprinkle with sliced almonds if desired. Serve immediately.

Chef's Tip
This goes well with fresh salad of raw cabbage and onion and flat breads with yogurt and cucumber dip.

Shakshuka: Poached Egg and Spicy Tomatoes
Tunisia

Eggs are more often associated with breakfast than as the main dish but the beauty of this recipe is that it can be adapted for either use in a meal. Shahshuka is widely eaten across North Africa and the Middle East where its aromatic flavour enhances the creamy texture of the poached eggs.

Serves 4

2 tablespoons olive oil • 1 large onion, sliced • 1 large red pepper, sliced • 4 garlic cloves, thinly, sliced • 1 tablespoon tomato paste • 1 tablespoon harissa • 1 teaspoon cumin • 1 teaspoon sugar • 400g tin chopped tomatoes • Salt and pepper to taste • 4 handfuls spinach • 6 large eggs • Fresh coriander, to garnish • Bread, fresh

Heat the oil in a large frying pan. Sauté the onions over a low heat for up to 10 minutes until soft and translucent.

Add the peppers and sauté for another 5 minutes until softening. Add the garlic, tomato paste, harissa and cumin. Cook for a minute then pour in the tinned tomatoes and sugar. Add salt and pepper to taste.

Simmer until the sauce is thickened, 10-20 minutes. If it becomes too thick add a little water. Stir in the spinach and cook until wilted.

Make 6 wells in the mixture and crack an egg into each one. Cover the pan and cook until the whites are set. This will take around 10 minutes. Serve sprinkled with chopped coriander.

Chef's Tip
For a fresher flavour use vine ripened tomatoes instead of tinned ones. Have some bread ready to mop up the juices.

Chicken Kabsa: Arabian Meat and Rice
Saudi Arabia

Traditional meat and rice dishes, referred to as Kabsa, or Al Kabsa, are popular in Saudi Arabia and surrounding countries at special occasions; particularly during Ramadan. After the sunset it is often a main element of Iftar; the meal that breaks the day's fasting. There are many different meat and rice recipes using chicken, lamb, beef or even goat or camel. This dish uses chicken but you can easily substitute any of the other meats listed above . Don't be put off by the length of the ingredients list, it is a relatively simple one-pot dish to prepare and cook.

Serves 4

3 tablespoons olive oil • 1 plum tomato, diced • 2 tablespoons tomato paste • 1 white onion, finely chopped • 1 tablespoon mixed spice • 1 teaspoon chilli powder • 4 cardamom pods • 4 large garlic cloves, crushed • 1 teaspoon ground cinnamon • 600ml vegetable stock • 2 dried limes • pinch of saffron • 400g basmati rice, washed and soaked • 500g chicken breast, cut into 3cm pieces • To garnish: fresh coriander, crushed pistachio nuts, almonds and pomegranate

Wash the rice under a cold tap using a sieve until the water runs clear and then soak it in cold water for 30 minutes. In a heavy pan on a medium heat, add half of the olive oil. Add the chicken in batches and brown on all sides. Remove the chicken.

In the same heavy pan add the rest of the olive oil and gently brown the onion. Add the plum tomatoes and tomato paste and stir until thickened. Add the chicken and any juices plus the mixed spice, chilli powder, cardamom pods, garlic, vegetable stock, dried limes and saffron. Bring to a slow simmer, cover and leave to cook for 30 minutes. If you can't find dried limes then use the zest and juice a fresh lime.

After 30 minutes drain the rice and add it to the pan, mixing it with the chicken. Bring it to the boil straight away and then lower the heat so it continues simmering gently. Cover and do not open the lid again for at least 20 minutes.

After 20 minutes open the lid and stir in the salt and pepper to taste. Leave with the lid off for a few minutes and then fluff up the rice with a fork. Garnish with chopped fresh coriander, crushed pistachio nuts, almonds and pomegranate.

Chef's Tip
Toast the crushed nuts in a dry pan over a medium heat for a minute or two for an extra nutty flavour.

Lahmacun: Beef Tortillas
Turkey, Northern Cyprus

Pronounced lak-maj-un, this is popular in Turkey and Northern Cyprus and is sometimes known as 'Turkish Pizza'. This is very easy and quick to make and cook and make a really tasty meal/snack.

Serves 3 or 4

250g lean ground beef • 1 large onion, finely chopped • 200g crushed tomatoes • 1 tablespoon tomato puree • 2 tablespoons dried parsley • ½ teaspoon cumin • ½ teaspoon black pepper • ¼ teaspoon chilli pepper (optional) • 1½ teaspoon salt • 6 flour tortillas • 2 lemons • A handful of fresh parsley • Greek style yogurt

Mix all the ingredients (except the tortillas) thoroughly in a bowl. Make sure you get your hands in there and give it a good squeeze. Leave the mixture in the fridge for 1 to 2 hours for the meat to absorb the flavour. With a spatula spread a thin layer of the mixture evenly on the tortillas.

Preheat the oven to 190°C and place 1 or 2 tortillas with ground beef on a tray on the third shelf from the top. As soon as it's in the oven, turn on the grill cook for 2 to 3 minutes, making sure not to burn the tortillas.

Once grilled, place the tortillas in a large pot on top of each other and close the lid to ensure they stay warm and soft. When all tortillas are cooked, place them on a plate and squeeze fresh lemon juice on top, a few sprigs of fresh parsley and a splodge of yogurt on the side.

Chef's Tip
Make sure you go the whole hog and throw in the chilli pepper!

Roasted Aubergine
Southern Turkey

A recipe from southern Turkey where aubergines often feature in home and village restaurant cooking. A healthy meal you can enjoy without guilt. Save the guilt for a bottle of white that you wash it down with.

Serves 4

**2 aubergines • 2 cloves garlic (grated) • 4 tablespoons
yoghurt • Juice of ½ lemon • 3 tablespoons extra virgin
olive oil • 1 teaspoon salt • 70g crushed walnuts or
almonds • Fresh mint or parsley to garnish**

Roast the aubergines in the oven at 200°C or under the grill until they are soft, turning upside down occasionally. Remove the skins of the aubergines and then mash in a food processor.

Sauté the aubergine with extra virgin olive oil and the garlic over a medium heat for about 4 to 5 minutes. Leave to cool for a couple of minutes.

Stir in the yoghurt once the mixture is cool together with the lemon or lime juice and salt. Place on a serving plate and sprinkle the crushed walnuts or almonds on top.

Dress it up with the fresh mint or parsley.

Chef's Tip
To go the full Mediterranean hog serve with warm pitta bread.

Shrimp with Olive Oil
Southern Turkey

A recipe from southern Turkey in the sunny Mediterranean.
Look at these ingredients: not much to make you feel guilty
about in there. Try this one with an pilsner beer and pretend
you are at a sea front bar with the water lapping at the rocks.

Serves 4

500g peeled shrimp or prawns • 1 onion, chopped • 250g mushrooms, washed • 1 carrot, sliced lengthways • 3 cloves garlic, finely chopped • 80ml olive oil • 2 tomatoes, diced • 1 large potato, diced • 1 tablespoon salt • ½ teaspoon black pepper • 120ml hot water • Fresh parsley for garnish

Place the olive oil and onion in a pot and sauté for about 3 minutes over a medium heat. Stir in the garlic and shrimp/ prawns and sauté for a further 2 minutes. Add the potatoes, carrot and mushroom and cook over a medium heat for 4 to 5 minutes.

Introduce the tomatoes, salt and hot water and bring to the boil, then simmer for about 20 minutes or until the potatoes are softened. Sprinkle with black pepper and garnish with parsley, stand back to admire your creation then tuck in.

Chef's Tip
This is best eaten with a fresh, crusty bread. This dish can form part of a 'tapas' style meal.

Ugali: Mashed Celeriac and Potatoes
West Africa

Ugali is a traditional mash eaten across the whole of West and Central Africa but the usual means of making it, with cassava or cornmeal, can produce a dish that is far too starchy for most western palates. I love ugali but it can be hard going so I have varied the recipe to include flavoursome ingredients such as sautéed leeks, celery, beetroots and walnuts. Ugali is often eaten on its own as a main course but I have added a sauce so that it makes a delicious vegetarian dinner. For those that want to experience the real thing, I have included a West African ugali recipe as a Chef's Tip.

Serves 4
**400g celeriac, peeled and cut into cubes • 400g large
potatoes, peeled and cut into large cubes • 2 garlic cloves,
chopped • 1 teaspoon whole peppercorns • 1 tablespoon
sea salt flakes • 2 bay leaves • 2 tablespoons rapeseed oil
or olive oil**

For the sauce
**1 tablespoon rapeseed oil • 1 garlic clove, chopped • 200g
raw beetroot, peeled and cut into very small cubes • 2
celery stalks, finely chopped • 2 leeks finely chopped • 60g
walnuts, finely chopped • Freshly ground pepper to taste**

Place the celeriac, potatoes, garlic, peppercorns, salt and bay
leaves into a large pan. Cover generously with water, bring to
a boil and then let it simmer for 30 minutes.

You can prepare the sauce whilst the vegetables are
simmering. Heat the oil in a sauté pan. To the heated oil, add
the garlic and beetroot and cook on low heat for five minutes.
Add the remaining vegetables and walnuts. Continue to cook
for another five minutes. Add salt and pepper to taste. Keep
the sauce warm.

Drain the vegetables which have now cooked for thirty
minutes and place in a big bowl. Discard the bay leaves. Now
add rapeseed or olive oil and mash, mixing everything well
together. Add pepper and salt to taste. Serve the mash with
the sauce on the side.

Chef's Tip
For traditional ugali cook 260g of cornmeal in 550ml of salted
boiling water. Stiring continually and mashing any lumps
that form. After 10 to 15 minutes mould into balls and serve.

Khoresht e Bademjan: Lamb and Aubergine Stew
Iran

This classic Persian recipe is sometimes prepared as a vegetarian dish but I prefer my recipes to have lamb in it but this can be omitted. Either way, you will not be disappointed.

Serves 6
2 large onions, peeled and thinly sliced • 2 cloves garlic, peeled and crushed • 1kg lamb shanks • Olive oil • 1 teaspoon salt • ¼ teaspoon freshly ground black pepper • 1 teaspoon turmeric • ½ teaspoon ground saffron dissolved in 4 tablespoons of hot water • 500ml of freshly squeezed tomato juice or a can of tomatoes • Juice from ½ lemon or 225g of unripe grapes • 4 tablespoons lime juice • 3 medium aubergines • 1 egg white • 1 teaspoon Persian allspice (optional)

Garnish
1 large onion, peeled and thinly sliced • 1 large tomato, peeled and left whole

Peel the aubergines and, if they are large, cut them lengthwise in quarters. Place them in a colander, sprinkle both sides with water and 2 tablespoons of salt. Set aside for 20 minutes then rinse them and pat dry with a kitchen paper towel.

In a non-stick pan, poor in 3 tablespoons of olive oil and bring it to a medium heat. Brown the onions and garlic and add the lamb shanks. Add salt, pepper, turmeric and saffron water.

Add the Persian allspice to the meat, mix well. Add 500ml of water to the meat and then the tomato juice and lime juice. Cover and simmer over low heat for 45 to 50 minutes.

Brush the aubergines on all sides with the egg white. In a non-stick skillet add 3 tablespoons of olive oil on medium-high heat and brown both sides of the aubergines. Set aside.

Preheat the oven to 180°C. Transfer the meat and sauce into a deep ovenproof casserole dish. Arrange the lamb shanks, sauce and unripe grapes (if used) and then place the aubergines on top. Cover and bake for 10 minutes, then remove the lid and bake another 10 minutes uncovered or until the aubergines are tender.

For the garnish bring 500ml of water to the boil in a kettle. Put the tomato in a bowl and make a little cross cut on top. Pour boiling water on the tomato and leave for 30-40 seconds, you will then be able to peel the skin of tomato very easily. Take a non-stick skillet, heat 2 tablespoons of oil on medium heat and brown the onion and tomato. Set the garnish aside.

Once cooked - take out of oven and pour garnish on top. Serve immediately from the same dish or keep warm in the oven until ready to serve.

Chef's Tip
Serve with steamed saffron plain rice.

Desserts

Banana and Chocolate Chip Cake
Dubai

When on holiday in Dubai my wife and I came across the most delicious banana cake at one of the fabulous beach hotels. After several attempts to find the perfect banana cake recipe, and after consuming lots of banana cake, this is the closest we have got to the perfect cake we had in Dubai.

Serves 4
2 large ripe bananas • ½ teaspoon vanilla flavouring •
175g butter • 225g granulated sugar • 275g self-raising
flour • ½ teaspoon bicarbonate of soda • 3 eggs, beaten •
100g milk chocolate chips

Grease and line two 8 inch diameter cake tins. Peel the bananas and mash until smooth with the vanilla flavouring.

Melt the butter and sugar in a saucepan until dissolved. Once this is done remove from the heat and stir in the flour and bicarbonate of soda.

Beat in the eggs and mashed banana and leave to cool slightly. Once the mixture has cooled stir in the chocolate chips.

Bake at 170°C for 35 minutes and then remove from the oven. Leave on a wire tray for a few minutes to cool. It can be eaten hot or cold.

Chef's Tip
Although not traditional in the Middle East, we have discovered that the cake goes well with fresh English custard. This makes an ideal after dinner treat.

Honey, Almonds and Vanilla Ice Cream
Iran

The heat and savoury food of the Middle East lends itself towards eating ice cream as a snack or dessert. This recipe is particularly popular in Iran and takes advantage of local ingredients to create a sweet, cooling dessert. Many Iranian restaurants will have this on their menu.

Serves 4
**225g sugar • 3 tablespoons honey • 5 tablespoons oil •
280g of unsalted almonds • ½ teaspoon ground saffron,
dissolved in 2 tablespoons of rose water • Several sprigs
of mint as required • Tub of good quality vanilla ice-
cream**

Heat the oil in a saucepan, once hot, add the honey and sugar and keep stirring until dissolved. Reduce heat if needed to avoid burning.

Reduce the heat to low and add the almonds to the mixture, stir from time to time, for about 2 minutes, until the mixture is golden and firm.

Add the saffron rose water mixture and cook for another 2 to 4 minutes, stirring occasionally, until the mixture is dark brown.

Place a bowl of ice water next to the cooker. Drop a spoonful of the hot almond mixture in the water. If it hardens quickly, the mixture is ready.

Spread a sheet of baking paper, place tablespoons of the mixture on paper, leaving space between each.

Allow the almonds to cool, and then remove from the paper.

Serve a scoop of the vanilla ice-cream in a bowl and add the cooled honey almond. Garnish with a sprig of mint.

Chef's Tip
A healthy and quick dessert option that can also be used as petit-four with coffee as well as a day-time snack.

Baklava
Turkey

Baklava is known across the world as a classic dessert (or snack) from the eastern Mediterranean. Most people I know assume that it is very difficult to make but in fact it is not complicated at all as the following recipe will demonstrate.

Makes 20 pieces
1 pack filo pastry • 250g butter, melted • 500g chopped nuts (walnuts and almonds) • 1 teaspoon ground cinnamon • 300g caster sugar • 12 tablespoons runny honey • 1 large piece lemon peel • 375ml water

First make the sauce. Boil the water and sugar until all the sugar is dissolved. Then add the honey and lemon. Simmer for around 15 minutes, remove from the heat, take out the lemon peel and allow to cool.

Preheat the oven to 180°C. Butter the bottom and sides of a 23 x 33 cm baking dish. Toss the chopped nuts in the cinnamon.

Unroll the filo pastry (only do this when you are ready to use it or it will dry out) then cover it with cling film and a damp tea towel. Cut the filo to the size of the baking dish. Place two sheets in the dish, painting the top one with melted butter. Repeat until you have eight layers.

Sprinkle 2 or 3 tablespoons of nuts onto the pastry, then cover with two more layers of pastry, topped with butter. Keep layering until all the nuts are used, finishing with six layers of filo.

Using your sharpest knife cut through MOST of the layers, to create 18 to 20 portions, but do not cut all the way through the bottom layer. Bake for around 50 minutes until golden brown and crisp.

Remove from the oven and pour the cooled sauce over the baklava. Leave uncovered somewhere to cool, then cut all the way through to serve.

Chef's Tip

It is important to keep the filo pastry damp before use and to cut the baklava before you bake it. To save time, do not paint butter onto each sheet but instead pour melted butter evenly over the whole dessert <u>after</u> you have cut it but before baking. The butter will soak into the dessert during baking creating the same overall taste.

Seffa de Couscous
Algeria, Tunisia, Morocco

Seffa de Couscous is a simple and delicious sweet dish popular in Tunisia, Morocco and Algeria as a dessert, particularly at special occasions. It is easy to make and you will surely love it.

Serves 4
150g couscous • A small handful of raisins • 4 to 6 dried figs, apricots, raisns and dates, diced • 2 to 3 teaspoons sugar • 1 orange, cut into cubes • 50g roasted almonds • 2 black/green cardamom seeds • Cinnamon • 1 tablespoon rose water

Prepare the Couscous by bringing 450ml of water to the boil in a pot. Poach the dried fruits in the boiling water for a few minutes. Add the couscous, sugar and the cardamom seeds and then cook according to the instructions on the couscous that you are using.

Toast the almonds by heating them in a pan on a medium to high heat until they just start to turn a golden colour. Add the rose water and orange cubes to the couscous.

Remove the cardamom seeds. Put the couscous onto a plate in the shape of a mound. Place the almonds on top of the couscous and sprinkle over some cinnamon.

Chef's Tip
Serve straight away so that it is still warm. You can add more sugar, dried fruits and orange to the dish if you prefer a sweeter taste, as the Moroccans do.

Malva Pudding
South Africa

Like much of South Africa's traditional cuisine, this recipe has its origins with the Dutch settlers at the Cape but has since spread to all parts of the country. Many families have their own variations and this one is mine.

Serves 4
For the pudding
65g white sugar •2 eggs •1 tablespoon apricot jam •1 tablespoon butter, melted •150g cake flour • 1 teaspoon baking powder • 1 teaspoon bicarbonate of soda • ¼ teaspoon salt • 60ml milk

For the syrup
75g butter • 130g white sugar • 120ml boiling water •
120ml cream with 1 teaspoon vanilla extract

Preheat an oven to 180°C and grease a large oven proof dish (e.g. a lasagne dish) with butter.

In a large bowl, beat the sugar and eggs together until they are soft and fluffy. In a separate bowl, sieve together the flour, baking powder, bicarbonate of soda, and salt.

Melt the butter gently in a heavy saucepan; make sure it does not boil. Add the jam and melted butter to the egg mixture and stir until absorbed.

Add the sifted ingredients into the wet ingredients and add the milk. Beat well. Pour the pudding mixture into the oven dish and bake until the pudding is brown and well risen. This will take approximately 30 to 45 minutes.

For the syrup. Melt the butter in the same saucepan as before. Add other ingredients to the pan and stir well. Pour the syrup over the pudding once it's out of the oven then leave to stand for a few minutes to allow the syrup to soak in. Serve warm with custard or ice cream.

Chef's Tip
This makes a great alternative to Christmas Pudding during the festive season.

Ma'amoul
Lebanon

Eid al-Fitr is the festival of breaking the fast, which marks the end of Ramadan across the Muslim world and ma'amoul, sometimes known as Eid cookies are a favourite treat. As Eid approaches, the smell of freshly baked ma'amoul spreads through every Middle Eastern household as these delicious shortbread snacks are prepared in readiness. These quick and easy recipes will provide everyone with a taste of Eid, although you need to fast through Ramadan if you want to truly experience the full effect.

Makes 20
For the dough
**400g plain flour • 1 teaspoon of baking powder • 1
tablespoon caster sugar, plus another 150g for dusting
• Pinch of salt • 200g unsalted butter • 2 tablespoons of
canola oil or rapeseed oil • 100ml of milk**

For a traditional date filling
**200g pitted dates • 2 tablespoons of water • Pinch of salt
• 50g finely chopped ginger • ½ teaspoon of finely grated
orange zest**

For a nut and raisin filling
**100g chopped toasted hazelnuts (or almonds and
pistachios) • 100g raisins • 3 tablespoons of apricot jam •
Pinch of salt**

For a quince and walnut filling
**150g chopped toasted walnuts • 100g quince jam • Pinch
of salt**

Turn up the oven to a medium heat, around 160°C.

Add the ingredients for each separate type of filling, to a
food processor and puree for a couple of minutes until evenly
combined. Then remove and puree the next filling, setting
each aside ready to add to your cookies.

Separately, add the flour, baking powder, caster sugar and
salt to a large bowl and mix lightly before adding the butter,
oil and milk. Mix well until the dough comes together but is
still slightly wet and don't overwork it.

Place your dough on a floured board and roll into 20
equally sized balls. Separately pick up your balls one at a time
and in the palm of your hand, press and pat each ball into

a small bowl shape. Place a rounded teaspoon of filling in the centre of your dough bowl and bring the edges up and around the filling.

Pinch the dough together to make a sealed ball and carefully roll your cookie ball between the palms of your hands to make a smooth round ball.

Press gently to flatten the cookie slightly and then place each cookie seam side down on a parchment-lined baking tray. Repeat with the remaining dough balls and when all 20 have been completed, you can either create your own decorative pattern by pricking them all with a fork or a wooden skewer or use a ma'amoul mould or spoon pressed down onto the top of each one.

Bake the cookies for about 25 to 30 minutes, until they are firm and slightly puffed. The tops should still be pale but the bottoms should be just beginning to turn golden. Place on a cooling tray and then dust generously with caster sugar and allow them to cool.

Chef's Tip
Take the trouble to buy ma'amoul moulds or spoons to give you the most authentic results.

Sables
Algeria

Algerian Sables are cookies made up of two pieces of shortbread with an exposed centre filling, traditionally using Jam. To look at they are very similar to the British Jammy Dodger but I'm sure you will agree the Algerian version has significantly better texture and taste. We are truly fortunate to have acquired this recipe on our travels and we hope your family can enjoy them as much as we continue to do.

Makes 25 Sables

For the Sables
250g of margarine or soft butter • 250g of granulated sugar • 1 large egg • 650g plain flour • ½ tea spoon of baking powder • 20ml of vanilla extract

For the filling and decoration
200g of strawberry jam or your preferred preserve • 200g of icing sugar

Preheat the oven to 170°C. Whisk the margarine and sugar together until light and fluffy. Add the egg and vanilla extract and mix together.

Add the baking power into the flour and then gently fold into the mixture until a soft dough is created. It should be very soft but not sticky. Add extra flour if you need to.

Roll out the dough on a lightly dusted surface until it is approx 3-4mm thick. You are now ready to put the tops and bottoms of your sable. If you have a selection of different cutters available you can be as creative as you wish. Traditionally, the top and bottom are round and have a diameter of approx 8cm, the top has a hole between 3 to 5 cm in the centre for the filling.

Place the tops and bottoms on a large foil lined baking tray and bake for just 8 minutes. The sables should be just set but still white. Allow the sables to cool by transferring to either a baking tray or cool plate until fully cooled.

Dust the sable tops with icing sugar.

Heat the preserve until bubbling hot and then allow to cool slightly before spooning ½ teaspoon onto the centre of the sable bottoms. Carefully then place the sable tops over the blobs of preserve and allow to set.

Chef's Tip
The sables should keep for up to 10 days in an airtight container although we've always eaten them long before then!

Balah El Sham
Algeria

Balah El Sham is a pastry with a dozen names, depending on where you are in the World. The name means Levant dates and these churro type fried choux fritters are popular across Middle East and much of Eastern European. Usually dipped in sugar syrup, they can also be stuffed with cream, chocolate, fruits and nuts or even served with ice cream. This recipe calls for a sugar syrup dip and then a roll in the nuts.

Makes Approx. 24
For the vanilla sugar syrup
**200g granulated sugar • 100ml water • ½ teaspoon of
lemon or orange juice • ½ teaspoon of vanilla extract**

For the Balah el Sham dough
**100g self raising flour • ¼ teaspoon salt • 100ml of
water • 100g unsalted butter • 6 eggs • 2 teaspoons of
vanilla extract • 500ml of vegetable oil, for deep frying
• Chopped nuts for rolling, particularly pistachios and
almonds**

Firstly, make the vanilla sugar syrup by bringing your water
to the boil in a small saucepan and then adding the sugar and
squeeze of lemon juice. Turn off the heat just before you add
these ingredients and keep stirring for around 10 minutes
until the syrup starts to thicken. At that point, then stir in the
vanilla and transfer to a large bowl to cool.

You're now ready to tackle your Balah El Sham, so rinse
out your saucepan and bring the water to the boil. Again,
turn off the heat and then add the butter and stir. Then add
the flour and salt and stir again until the mixture turns to a
thick dough. Let it cool fully and then add the vanilla extract
and the eggs one at a time, making sure each is mixed before
adding the next.

For best results, then transfer the dough to a pastry bag
fitted with a star tip. If you don't have one, then you can roll
and chop but your results will be less visually appealing. If
you're going to make these regularly, then get a bag with a 16
point star tip.

Bring your frying oil almost up to temperature but not quite to the boil. Then pipe the dough directly into the oil and snip off approximately 6cm at a time with a pair of scissors. If your oil is boiling the fritters will cook too quickly and will be less puffy.

Cook your Balah El Sham in groups of 6 or 8 at a time and don't be tempted to put too many in at once. Make sure you allow the temperature of your oil to drop between batches. Once cooked to a golden glow, remove your fritters and drain on paper towels. Don't let them cool completely as you need to dunk them in the sugar syrup before they do.

Once dunked, either roll them with your chopped nuts or sprinkle from a height if you prefer. Allow them to cool fully on a wire tray before eating.

Chef's Tip
Enhance the flavour by eating your Balah el Sham with cream or ice cream.

Koeksisters
South Africa

Koeksisters (pronounced 'cook sister') are syrup infused twisted doughnuts that originate from South Africa. We are not sure where our recipe originated, it has passed down through our family and has been a favourite for many generations. These would traditionally be eaten at breakfast but are delicious at any time of the day. As they are deep fried its perhaps best kept for special occasions!

Makes Approx. 21
For the Spicy Syrup
400g of granulated sugar • 1¼ teaspoons cream of tartar
• 1 tablespoon chopped ginger • Freshly squeezed lemon
juice (half lemon) • 1 cinnamon stick • 240ml water

For the Dough
100g corn flour • 180g plain flour • 2½ teaspoons baking
powder • ¾ teaspoon salt • 2 tablespoons of granulated
sugar • 120ml milk • 1 large egg • 25g butter

Firstly to make the syrup, you need to add the water, sugar and ginger into a small saucepan and heat on a low until it boils and all of the sugar has dissolved, then allow to simmer for about 10 minutes, stirring occasionally. Then remove from the heat and stir in the cream of tartar, lemon juice and cinnamon stick. Allow to cool and then refrigerate until ready to use.

To make the dough you should combine the plain flour, corn flour, sugar, baking powder and salt into a large mixing bowl, before adding all of the wet ingredients (milk and egg) followed by the butter. Work the mixture together and knead several times until all the ingredients have been incorporated before leaving it to rest for approx 30 minutes.

Roll out the dough on a lightly dusted surface until it is approx 3-4 mm thick. Use a knife to cut into thin strips and then shorter strips, no less than 15 cm long. Take three strands of dough and stretch them out carefully until they are of an even thickness all the way down before pinching together at one end. Then, take the left strand and cross it over the middle strand, take the right strand and cross it over the middle strand and repeat to braid to the desired length (typically about 15 cm) before pinching together to seal the end.

Pour vegetable oil into a large saucepan, until it is at least 10 cm deep and heat to approx 220°C.

Put about three Koeksisters in the pan at a time and fry on both sides until they are golden in colour. As soon as you remove the Koeksisters from the hot oil place them directly in the cooled syrup. It is important that the syrup remains cool so be sure to keep refrigerated in between batches.

Place the syrup coated Koeksisters in the fridge to cool before eating. Enjoy!

Chef's Tip
To test if the oil is hot enough put a small 'drop' of batter into the oil. If it is not hot enough, the batter will stay at the bottom of the pan rather than rising to the top.

Makrout Lâassel
Algeria

Makrout, which is Arabic for diamond-shaped, is a traditional North African semolina cookie. Originating in Tunisia and usually with a date filling, Makrout Lâassel is an Algerian version with an almond filling. These can be eaten without dip but for a more authentic flavour, these cookies should be dipped and even double dipped in honey.

Makes 6 or 7 Pieces
For the dough
750g semoule moyen (medium grained semolina) •
25g butter • 125g oil • 75g plain flour • pinch of salt • 1
tablespoon of vanilla powder or 3 or 4 drops of vanilla
extract or essence • 120ml of warm water (preferably
maz'har - orange blossom water)

For the filling
500g of ground almonds • 250g caster sugar • 1 teaspoon
of cinnamon • 1 tablespoon of vanilla powder • Vegetable
oil for frying • Honey for dipping

Melt the butter and add it to large mixing bowl, together with the oil. Then add the semolina and salt and mix well. Rub the grains of semolina between your fingers so that they all become well coated with the butter and oil mixture.

Once well mixed, cover the bowl and set aside to rest for at least two hours. But overnight is even better. In the morning, the dough should be like a wet oily sand consistency.

Add all the ingredients for the filling to a bowl and mix well with a spoon, bringing the mixture together to form a large ball. Tip onto a board and cut the ball in two and then roll each piece to form two logs.

Take your semolina dough and slowly add the blossom water. Mix well but don't overwork. You are looking for a smooth, flexible dough that forms into a ball easily. Again take your ball and cut in half and roll into two logs, only this time you then flatten your logs until they are large enough to wrap around your almond filling.

Place the almond filling roll in the centre of each flattened semolina dough and roll the dough around the filling nice and tight. Join the two edges together by pinching along the length, then turn your filled roll over so that it is seam side down and flatten slightly.

You then need to cut your filled semolina roll diagonally into 6 or 7 separate Makrout pieces. Use a fork or a knife to put a pattern into each piece and then set aside, whilst you bring a pan of oil up to temperature. Separately in another pan you should also slowly heat your dipping honey.

Add the Makrout to your oil in threes or fours at a time and fry until golden. Then remove and place on a paper towel to cool and drain. Once cooled, place each Makrout separately in the honey for a minute or so to allow it to absorb some of the honey. Then drain and repeat so that each Makrout gets two goes in the honey.

This recipe can be prepared in advance and served as a snack or at the end of a meal.

Chef's Tip
Your Makrout are best eaten whilst still fresh but will last 2 or 3 days.

Also available from First de Sales

Modern Verse
- Poetry for Now
- Poetry for Now Too

Real Life Stories
- A Day in the Life: Real Life Travel Stories
- Another Day in the Life: Extraordinary Real Life Stories
- A Further Day in the Life: Real Life Adventure Stories

Writing Skills
- Speech Writing for Every Occasion

Food and Drink
- Cocktails, Mocktails and Smoothies
- Simple World Cuisine
- Simple European Cuisine
- Simple British Cuisine
- Simple American Cuisine
- Simple Asian and Indian Cuisine